BOMBERS

MARK DARTFORD

Lerner Publications Company
Minneapolis

Lerner Publications Company.
A division of Lerner Publishing Group
241 First Avenue North
Minneapolis, MN 55401 U.S.A.

Website address: www.lernerbooks.com

Library of Congress Cataloging-in-Publication Data

Dartford, Mark.
 Bombers / by Mark Dartford.
      p. cm.—(Military hardware in action)
Includes index.
Summary: Discusses the military use of aorcraft to drop bombs and describes the development of particular kinds of bombers.
  ISBN 0–8225–4705–8 (lib. bdg.)
1. Bombers —Juvenile literature. 2. Armored vehicles,
3. Military—Juvenile literature. [1. Bombers 2. Airplanes, Military.] I. Title. II Series.
  UG1242.B6 D37 2003
  623.7'463—dc21   2002011854

Printed in China
Bound in the United States of America
1 2 3 4 5 6 – OS – 08 07 06 05 04 03

This book uses black and yellow chevrons as a decorative element on some headers. They do not point to other elements on the page.

Contents

Introduction

High in the sky, thin vapor trails drift from the horizon. Below, sirens wail. People drop what they are doing and rush to the nearest shelter. The bombers above unleash their deadly cargo. Moments later, the earth rocks as bombs strike the ground, shattering buildings and shaking morale.

DEADLY CARGO

U.S. Air Force Boeing B52s take off on a mission against terrorist camps in the mountains of Afghanistan. These actions took place during Operation Enduring Freedom in 2002.

>> **strafed** = machine-gunned the ground from the air

World War I

When World War I (1914–1918) broke out in Europe in 1914, military forces on all sides started to use airplanes for observation and to attack enemy positions. At first, scout planes dropped small bombs or **strafed** ground troops and airfields. By 1917 aircraft were bringing the war to ordinary people in cities and towns. German zeppelin airships and Gotha bombers raided enemy cities. The Germans hoped to scare the civilian population into surrendering.

DOUHET DOCTRINE

After World War I, most political and military leaders believed that bombers could win wars by blasting enemy industries, railroads, and cities and by terrorizing the population. Fast, all-metal, **monoplanes** replaced the early wood-and-fabric **biplanes**. This belief was summed up in the "Douhet Doctrine," named for an Italian officer. He claimed that the bomber—high above the reach of ground artillery and able to evade fighters—"would always get through."

BIG BOMBERS

The first strategic bombers were multi-engined biplanes, like the British Handley Page HP4. They flew long distances, dropping large bomb loads mainly on urban targets.

biplane = double wing airplane

World War II

In 1939 Germany invaded Poland and started World War II (1939–1945). The Germans used Junkers Ju87 Stuka dive bombers and long-range Heinkel He111s to strike airfields and cities. As the war spread, country after country collapsed under German blitzkrieg (lightning war) attacks.

TERROR DIVER

A Ju87 Stuka dives vertically. The plane was fitted with a wailing siren to terrify its victims. The Ju87 was effective as a terror weapon, but it was no match for a fast and well-armed fighter plane.

Pacific Theater

Japan's attack on Pearl Harbor in the Hawaiian Islands brought the United States into World War II in 1941. As the tide of the war turned, huge formations of Allied long-range bombers struck industrial cities in Japan and Germany.

Jet Age

Long-range jet bombers were developed in the **Cold War** period of the 1950s and 1960s. Western democracies faced Soviet and Chinese Communists in a standoff to win world influence. Each side had enough bomb power to destroy the opposition. This was called Mutual Assured Destruction, or MAD for short. Each side recognized that attacking the other would bring destruction upon itself.

THE BOEING KEEPS GOING

A Boeing B52 launches a Joint Direct Attack Munition **(JDAM)**. B52s have been flying for more than half a century.

The Bomber's Role

A bomber's job is to strike at targets on the surface. These can be frontline troops. Other targets include factories, stockyards, roads, and railroad stations far from the battle zone. Vessels at sea are also prime targets. Strike aircraft carry many different kinds of bombs, rockets, and missiles to do their job.

ROAD TO DESTRUCTION

Remains of Iraqi armor lie on a desert road after bombing attacks during the 1991 Persian Gulf War.

SWINGING INTO ACTION

The B1 Lancer bomber has swing-wing variable geometry. This means it can sweep back its wings for supersonic, or faster-than-sound, flight.

All Shapes and Sizes

There are many different kinds of fixed-wing strike aircraft. Heavy bombers carry big loads at high altitudes over long distances. They often bomb large areas. They are also called strategic bombers. The dive bombers of World War II launched smaller **munitions** at pinpoint targets. Modern equivalents of the dive bombers are called tactical strike aircraft. Torpedo bombers were developed specially for attacking shipping.

TACTICAL STRIKE

Tactical targets include troops, armor, and ships. Strike aircraft often attack at low levels.

STRATEGIC STEALTH

The B2 Spirit bomber can penetrate deep into enemy territory, carrying a large quantity of bombs and munitions.

STRATEGY AND TACTICS

Bombing missions are usually either strategic or tactical. Strategic bombers attack an enemy's **infrastructure**, targets such as factories, cities, or communications routes. Tactical aircraft strike smaller targets, usually inside the battle zone. Many strike aircraft operate from aircraft carriers, which can bring them close to the combat zone.

The Nuclear Deterrent

The **atomic bombs** dropped on the Japanese cities of Hiroshima and Nagasaki in 1945 marked the end of World War II and the beginning of the nuclear age. Until **intercontinental missiles** arrived, bombers were the only means of nuclear delivery. By 1950 the United States, Britain, France, the Soviet Union, and China all possessed atomic bombs. The United States, Britain, and the Soviet Union built jet airplanes capable of intercontinental delivery.

STRATOJET

The U.S. Air Force B47 Stratojet was the world's most advanced strategic nuclear bomber of the 1950s and 1960s. Stratojets remained in use until 1966.

>> **atomic bomb** – a nuclear weapon of mass destruction

LITTLE BOY

Little Boy was the name given to the type of atomic bomb dropped on Hiroshima near the end of World War II. Modern nuclear weapons are mainly confined to missiles and submarines. Modern bombers drop precision-guided munitions on carefully selected targets.

Getting in First

GROUNDED

During Operation Desert Storm in 1991, the Iraqi air force was wiped out while most of its aircraft were still on the ground.

An important job for the tactical bomber airplane is the first strike capability. This means taking out the enemy's main defenses, such as fighter aircraft or anti-aircraft artillery, before they can be used. In operations against Iraq in 1991 and in the war against terrorists in 2001–2002, U.S strike aircraft destroyed enemy defenses to assure safe passage for troop-carrying transports.

The Bomber Crew

The earliest bomber airplanes of World War I had a crew of just one or two. By World War II, heavy bombers like the **B29** carried crews of up to fourteen. Modern strike aircraft, with the assistance of navigation and target-finding technology, have come full circle. Strategic bombers like the B1 need only three or four crewmembers. Smaller strike aircraft can carry **ordnance** loads like those of World War II bombers but using only a single pilot.

ALL IN ONE

The A7 Corsair II's pilot is also its navigator and weapons officer. The Corsair II has more hitting power than a World War II heavy bomber.

Inside the Bomber

WORLD WAR II CREW

A single British heavy night bomber of World War II carried a crew of eight men—pilot, flight engineer, bomb aimer, navigator, radio operator, mid-upper gunner, and rear gunner.

MODERN CREW

The B1 Lancer has a crew of four. They are the pilot/commander (*shown, left*), co-pilot/flight mechanic (*shown, right*), the offensive systems operator, and the defensive systems operator. There is an additional folding rear seat for a systems instructor on noncombat training flights. The systems operators sit behind the flight crew.

Building Skills

All aircrew recruits to the U.S. armed forces learn to fly in small, single-engine airplanes. They start with **turboprops** and move up to jets. Pilots and navigators then continue through larger and more complicated machines until they are ready to handle the high-tech hard-hitters with confidence.

BASIC FLYING TRAINING

This is where jet flying skills start, with one-on-one instruction in a T37 two-seat training airplane.

U.S. AIR FORCE

Virtual World

STEALTH BOX

This state-of-the-art bomber simulator looks like a big box on the outside. But inside it copies the interior of the real thing. The simulator tilts in all directions, to give a sense of flying motion.

Ground simulation **virtual reality** is a major part of modern flying and combat mission training. A student can practice handling skills and response without the cost or danger of actual flight. Experienced crews can also keep their skills sharp in the simulator.

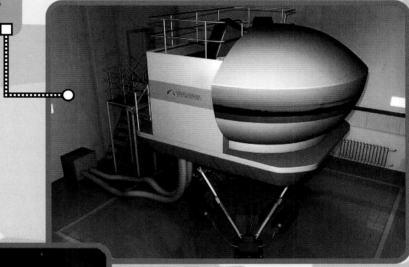

NIGHT FLYING ANYTIME

A pilot practices a night mission inside a B1 Lancer simulator. All the instrument readouts are realistic. Moving scenery is projected onto screens in front of the cockpit "window."

INSTRUCTOR'S VIEW

"[The simulator] lets you practice the procedures and mission flow before actually flying the mission—kind of like scrimmaging before a football game."

Captain C. Cunningham, weapons officer,
Langley Air Force Base

Bomber Weapons

Most strike aircraft carry either "dumb" bombs or "smart" bombs. Free-falling dumb, or gravity, bombs are similar to those dropped in World War II. Smart bombs have their own precision guidance systems. Some are TV-guided, with a camera in the bomb and a monitor with radio control in the aircraft. Others, like the Paveways, are guided by lasers and Global Positioning System **(GPS).** Many smart bombs have control surfaces, so they glide to the target.

HORNET'S NEST

U.S. Air Force F15 Eagle drops Paveway Laser Guided Bombs (LGBs). The F15 can carry a wide range of munitions, including varieties of bombs, anti-ship missiles, and anti-personnel mines.

LASER POWER

To hit difficult targets like bridges, U.S. and Allied forces used laser-guided bombs in the 1990s. Their efforts were part of the UN-sponsored campaign against Serbian forces in Bosnia.

FLYING BOMBS

Flying bombs are fitted with small winglets and directional guidance sensors. They steer the bomb precisely onto a selected target. A laser beam is reflected off the target. This creates a path toward which the bomb steers.

DIRECT HIT

Bombs have different **warheads,** depending on the job they have to do. During Operation Desert Storm in 1991 and anti-terrorist operations in Afghanistan in 2002, laser-guided U.S. Bunker Buster BLU113 bombs were dropped to penetrate enemy hard shelters, like these Iraqi aircraft hangars in 1991.

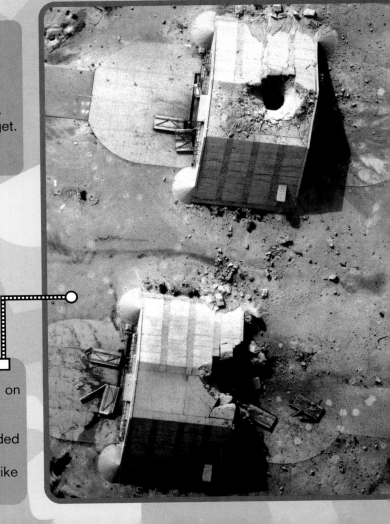

Groundbreakers

In the early 2000s, U.S. forces dropped BLU118 fuel-air bombs on forces operating from tunnels in the Afghan mountains. The BLU118 bomb is a powerful bunker-penetration weapon that collapses underground structures. It lights oxygen in the trapped air, burning everything inside. Strike airplanes also carry low-level attack ordnance. Cannons, rockets, and air-to-ground missiles like the Maverick are effective against small, individual targets such as tanks.

DEADLY CARGO

Bomb loaders prepare a B52 for its mission over Afghanistan.

Guns, Rockets, and Missiles

TWO IN ONE

The F14 Tomcat is a fighter with added strike capability. **Pylons** beneath the wings and **fuselage** carry a combination of bombs, missiles, and long-range fuel tanks. It is also fitted with a 20mm cannon for close defense.

FLYING GUN

The A10 Thunderbolt II "Warthog" is a specialty anti-tank airplane. Its body is built around a powerful tank-busting rapid-fire cannon. It also has underwing pylons stacked with ordnance.

Bombers in Action

During World War I, bombing raids by German zeppelin airships and clumsy biplanes had little effect on the brutal ground war. In the 1930s, air raids on civilian populations during the Spanish Civil War and the Japanese invasion of China caused much destruction and terror among the population. The world woke up to the full potential of aerial bombardment.

World War II

Bombing affected every theater of the war, from the German blitzkrieg, through the Allied bomber raids over Germany, to the atomic bombs dropped on Japan. To cripple the Nazi war machine, industrial regions of Germany were **carpet bombed** by huge formations of Allied heavy bombers.

FLYING FORTRESS

The B17 Flying Fortress led the daylight bombing campaign in Europe.

NAZI INDUSTRY ABLAZE

In October 1943, U.S. B17s based in England launched massive raids on the Schweinfurt **ball-bearing** factory in Germany. Ball-bearings were vital to German industrial and military production.

LESSON LEARNED

Schweinfurt raiders en route in broad daylight. The attack succeeded, but many of the B17s were lost, which forced a review of long-distance bombing tactics.

Bombers in Action

In April 1942, just four months after Pearl Harbor, the U.S. counter-attacked targets in Japan. Sixteen long-range B25 bombers commanded by Lieutenant Colonel James H. Doolittle took off from the aircraft carrier USS *Hornet*. They crossed 500 miles of Pacific Ocean, dropped their bombs on Tokyo, and continued on toward China. Fifteen ran out of fuel. One landed in the Soviet Union.

DOOLITTLE'S DARING DEED

Two-engine B25s were changed to take off from a carrier deck normally used by smaller bombers. Doolittle's raid humiliated Japan's military and political leaders.

Pacific War

In the Pacific, U.S. forces fought through the Ryukyu Islands, until they came within striking distance of the Japanese mainland. Air raids on Tokyo almost completely destroyed Japan's capital city. The bombers dropped **incendiaries,** since most of the city's buildings were made of wood.

TOKYO IN TATTERS

Only Tokyo's masonry buildings survived constant attacks by U.S. bombers.

BOMB THAT CHANGED THE WORLD

On August 6, 1945, *Enola Gay*, a B29 commanded by Colonel Paul W. Tibbetts Jr, dropped the world's first atomic bomb on Hiroshima. It detonated over the city, destroying everything and everyone within a 10-mile radius. Roughly 70,000 people died immediately. Many more died later from the effects of **radiation**.

radiation

Bombers in Action

In December 1972, during the Vietnam War (1965–1975), U.S. forces launched a massive bombing campaign against North Vietnam. **Code-named** Linebacker II, it was the largest bombing offensive of the conflict. Over 11 days, 40,000 tons of high explosives were dropped from B52s onto major targets, including the cities of Hanoi and Haiphong. The overall objective was to bring North Vietnam's leaders back to the peace talks being held in Paris.

VIETNAM VETERAN

The Douglas A1 Skyraider low-level strike airplane, popularly called "Spad," served throughout the Vietnam War. First built in 1944, it was used in World War II and the Korean War (1950–1953) by the U.S. Navy, Air Force, and Marine Corps. Even in the jet age, prop-driven Skyraiders were still being flown in the late 1970s.

LINEBACKER II

In 1972 over 350 B52s took part in the high-altitude night attacks. The campaign seemed to work. The peace talks in Paris resumed in January 1973.

A string of U.S. Navy A7 Corsair IIs lines up to take on fuel from an **airborne tanker**. They were part of Operation Desert Storm. This coalition of international forces led by the United States forced Iraq to leave neighboring Kuwait. Iraq had occupied Kuwait in 1990, defying international law.

Enduring Freedom

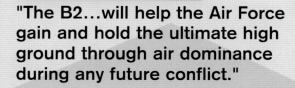 B2 Spirit bombers played a key part in operations against terrorist forces hiding in Afghanistan in 2001–2002. Able to enter enemy airspace without being seen, these airplanes were also vital in knocking out enemy fighter and anti-aircraft defenses.

HERE TO STAY

"The B2…will help the Air Force gain and hold the ultimate high ground through air dominance during any future conflict."

General J. Jumper,
U.S. Air Force Air Combat Command

UP CLOSE

With a potential range of 10,000 miles, the high-altitude B2 closes on its target unseen.

Finding the Target

A bomber works like an unwelcome delivery service. It picks up at point A and delivers to point B. But the process in between—of first locating the target, then hitting it accurately—demands a skilled crew and technological know-how.

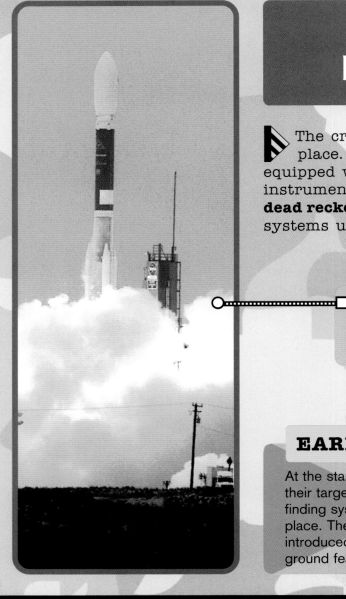

Satellite Navigation

The crew's first job is to get to the right place. All modern military airplanes are equipped with satellite-based GPS navigation instruments. GPS is more accurate than the **dead reckoning** and ground-signal station systems used in the past.

LIFT OFF

A Navstar GPS satellite lifts off aboard a U.S. Air Force Delta II rocket at Cape Canaveral, Florida.

EARLY DAYS

At the start of World War II, most bombers reached their targets using air charts. Later, radio direction finding systems helped the bombers go to the right place. Then, simple **cathode ray sets** were introduced. These gave the crew an outline image of ground features below, even through cloud cover.

HIT AND MISS

"I can't recall more than one or two occasions where I could genuinely say that I hit the target. We went to Bremen [in Germany] ... a thousand bombers there and we do nothing ... Terrific disappointment!"

Royal Air Force navigator, World War II

LOW-TECH RAIDERS

The bomb aimer/navigator in this German Heinkel He111 in 1940 only had charts and a mechanical bombsight.

NORDEN BOMBSIGHT

The U.S. Norden bombsight was the most accurate bombsight of World War II. It included a simple computer that calculated the exact moment to release the bombs.

Finding the Target

Reconnaissance (exploration of an area to gain information) is a vital part of target finding. Photographs are taken from high-altitude spy planes, like the U2 and SR71. Modern space satellite imaging can identify a target as small as a single vehicle deep inside enemy territory. Modern satellites and aircraft also use **infrared** and **thermal imaging** to find objects like buildings or tanks, even through thick cloud or treetops.

Six-Day Wonder

In 1967 Arab and Israeli air forces fought the Six-Day War. Israel had accurate aerial information and equally accurate first strikes. These strikes put the Egyptian and Jordanian air forces out of action at the start of the war.

SKY-HIGH EYE

The U2 can fly at more than 80,000 feet, too high to be seen from the ground.

>> infrare

Unmanned radio-controlled aircraft can send back TV pictures and other information. They are relatively cheap and safe for short-distance reconnaissance missions.

SO OTHERS CAN FOLLOW

Specialty aircraft are used for close-in target marking. Rockets and flares identify the site for follow-up strikes by air or ground ordnance. The OV10 Bronco successfully picked out targets in various conflicts from Vietnam to the Persian Gulf.

hermal in

Enemies of the Bomber

Bombers are at risk of attack from other airplanes, from anti-aircraft artillery, and from missiles.

FLAK

During World War II, Germany developed **flak,** a very effective artillery system based on its 88mm anti-tank gun. It was much feared by bomber crews. First, the target aircraft was "coned" by two or three searchlight beams or tracked by radar. Shells with **proximity fuses** burst around the aircraft, peppering it with shrapnel or scoring a direct hit.

LOOKING UP

German flak guns wait for the daylight raiders to appear.

Modern Missile Menace

DEADLY AERIAL COMBINATION

F15 Eagles launch AIM Sidewinder air-to-air missiles.

Modern bombers are most likely to be hit by missiles. Anti-aircraft missiles can be launched from the ground, from other airplanes, or from ships. Missiles may be radar guided, laser guided, wire guided, or infrared heat seeking.

STING IN THE TAIL

The FIM92A Stinger missile is made in the United States. It is a handheld infantry anti-aircraft rocket with a reach of over 11,000 feet. Its infrared sensor locks on to the heat from an airplane's jet tailpipe.

SEA SPARROW

A ship-launched Sea Sparrow anti-aircraft missile. Sea Sparrow is a high-velocity missile that can also attack incoming missiles.

Defenses

Strike aircraft have several defenses against missile attack. The first is identification, friend or foe (IFF). This radar-detection system alerts the crew when a missile has targeted their plane. The crew can switch on electronic countermeasures (ECM), which can jam an enemy missile-guidance system.

TELLTALE TAILFIN

The Grumman EA6 Prowler stores a range of sophisticated ECM equipment in its bulging tail.

SKY CHAPARRAL

A tracked M113 with radar-guided Chaparral SAM surface-to-air missiles is ready for action during the 1991 Persian Gulf War.

Defensive Stealth

> An important modern defensive technique is [stealth] technology. Stealth uses **nonreflective** mater[ial to] make an airplane invisible to enemy detection systems.

B2 SPIRIT

The B2 has a very **low radar profile**, with engines baffled (muffled) against heat detection. It can attack with the vital element of surprise.

Bombers and Strike Aircraft

There are many different kinds of fixed-wing strike aircraft built and operated all over the world. Heavy strategic bombers can fly long distances. Small, single-engine airplanes can operate from jungle and mountain airstrips.

A4 SKYHAWK

The McDonnell Douglas A4 Skyhawk was introduced in the early 1960s. It has been continually upgraded since and is in service with the Air National Guard and with many foreign countries.

Details:
Crew: 1
Length: 41 ft. 9 in.
Wingspan: 27 ft. 6 in.
Propulsion: 1 x 9,300 lb. thrust **turbojet**
Max Speed: 700 mph at sea level
Ceiling: 40,000 ft.
Armament: 2 x 20mm cannons, 8,200 lb. bomb load

A6 INTRUDER

The Grumman A6 Intruder is an all-weather, carrier-borne strike aircraft. It was the main strike aircraft of the U.S. Navy and Marine Corps during the Vietnam War. It continued in service to the end of the 1900s.

Details:
Crew: 2
Length: 54 ft. 9 in.
Wingspan: 53 ft.
Propulsion: 2 x 9,300 lb. thrust turbojets
Max Speed: 644 mph at sea level
Ceiling: 42,000 ft.
Armament: 18,200 lb. bomb load, including iron bombs and anti-ship missiles

>> **turbojet** = a conventional jet engine, with compressors

TORNADO GR1

The Panavia Tornado GR1 was designed by a British, German, and Italian group. It has variable geometry wings, with fly-by-wire (computerized) control systems. The GR1 is a low-level, high-load strike version of the multirole combat airplane.

Details:
Crew: 2
Length: 54 ft. 11 in.
Wingspan: 45 ft. 8 in. (spread)
Propulsion: 2 x 16,800 lb. thrust afterburning **turbofans**
Max Speed: 1453 mph at sea level
Ceiling: 50,000 ft.
Armament: 2 x 20mm cannons, 20,000 lb. bomb load, including dumb bombs and missiles

>> **turbofan** – a jet engine with extra fans that increase its power

Bombers and Strike Aircraft

A7 CORSAIR II

The Vought A7 Corsair II had an outstanding reputation for carrying heavy loads. Both the U.S. Navy and Air Force operated these all-weather strike aircraft before they were replaced by the F/A18 Hornet.

Details:
Crew: 1
Length: 46 ft.
Wingspan: 38 ft. 9 in.
Propulsion: 1 x 23,400 lb. thrust turbofan
Max Speed: 661 mph at sea level
Ceiling: 40,000 ft.
Armament: 1 x 20mm gun, 15,000 lb. bomb load

>> vectored thrust – jet nozzles that can rotate to boost turning rate

AV8 HARRIER

The AV8 Harrier is a joint development between McDonnell Douglas and British Aerospace. It was developed in the United States for use by the U.S. Marine Corps and has **vectored thrust** vertical takeoff and landing (VTOL) capability.

Details:
Crew: 1
Length: 46 ft. 4 in.
Wingspan: 30 ft. 4 in.
Propulsion: 1 x 15,000 lb. thrust turbofan
Max Speed: 690 mph at sea level
Ceiling: 50,000 ft.
Armament: 2 x 25mm cannons, 9,200 lb. bomb and/or missile load

ALPHA

The Alpha jet is built by France and Germany. It is a **subsonic,** low-cost strike aircraft able to operate from unpaved airstrips. There are training and tactical strike models of this multirole airplane.

Details:
Crew: 2
Length: 40 ft. 3 in.
Wingspan: 30 ft.
Propulsion: 2 x 5,952 lb. thrust turbofans
Max Speed: 725 mph at sea level
Ceiling: 50,000 ft.
Armament: 1 x 20mm cannon, 7,000 lb. bomb and/or missile load

Bombers and Strike Aircraft

F111 AARDVARK

The General Dynamics F111 Aardvark was designed as a long-range bomber and strike aircraft for the U.S. Navy and Air Force. It features variable-geometry wings, with a large armament capability. It has mostly been replaced by the B1.

Details:
Crew: 2
Length: 73 ft. 6 in.
Wingspan: 63 ft. (spread)
Propulsion: 2 x 25,100 lb. thrust afterburning turbofans
Max Speed: 1653 mph at sea level
Ceiling: 59,000 ft.
Armament: 1 x 20mm Vulcan cannon, 31,500 lb. bomb load, including nuclear bombs

HAWK 200

The British Aerospace Hawk 200 is a single-seat multirole combat aircraft (MRCA) based on the Hawk 100 **advanced trainer**. It serves with the Royal Air Force and has been sold worldwide.

Details:
Crew: 1
Length: 37 ft. 3 in.
Wingspan: 32 ft. 8 in.
Propulsion: 1 x 5845 lb. thrust turbofan
Max Speed: 660 mph at sea level
Ceiling: 45,000 ft.
Armament: 6615 lb. bomb load, including rockets

>> advanced trainer – an airplane for combat training

TU16 "BADGER"

The Tupolev Tu16, designated "Badger" by **NATO,** is one of Russia's longest-serving heavy bombers. It has a history similar to the B52. Although production ceased in the 1960s, many remain operational.

Details:
Crew: 7
Length: 114 ft. 2 in.
Wingspan: 108 ft. 3 in.
Propulsion: 2 x 20,920 lb. thrust turbojets
Max Speed: 650 mph at sea level
Ceiling: 49,000 ft.
Armament: 7 x 23mm cannons, 19,800 lb. bomb load, including nuclear bombs

Bombers and Strike Aircraft

S3 VIKING

The Lockheed S3 Viking is an all-weather, carrier-borne specialty anti-submarine strike airplane. It was designed to replace the U.S. S2 Tracker and offers an improved armament load plus upgraded **avionics.**

Details:
Crew: 4
Length: 53 ft. 4 in.
Wingspan: 68 ft. 8 in.
Propulsion: 2 x 9,275 lb. thrust turbofans
Max Speed: 184 mph at sea level
Ceiling: 35,000 ft.
Armament: various bombs, depth charges, anti-ship missiles, and flare launchers

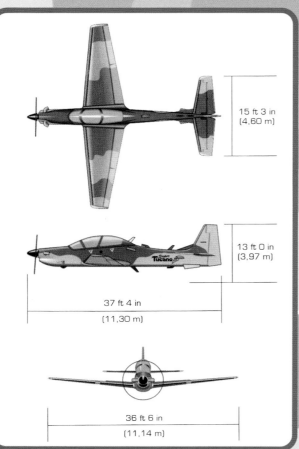

15 ft 3 in
(4,60 m)

13 ft 0 in
(3,97 m)

37 ft 4 in
(11,30 m)

36 ft 6 in
(11,14 m)

EMB314 SUPER TUCANO

The Embraer EMB314 ALX Super Tucano is a light strike aircraft developed by Brazil for border observation and **counter-insurgency** roles. It is exported as a strike trainer to several other countries.

Details:
Crew: 1
Length: 37 ft. 4 in.
Wingspan: 36 ft. 6 in.
Propulsion: 1 x 1600 hp turboprop
Max Speed: 557 mph at sea level
Ceiling: 35,000 ft.
Armament: 2 x 12.7mm MGs, 3300 lb. bomb and missile load

TU160 "BLACKJACK"

The Tupolev Tu160, designated "Blackjack" by NATO, is Russia's answer to the B1 Lancer. It has variable geometry wings and is the largest bomber currently in service in the world.

Details:
Crew: 4
Length: 177 ft. 6 in.
Wingspan: 182 ft. 9 in.
Propulsion: 4 x 50,580 lb. thrust turbojets
Max Speed: 1380 mph at sea level
Ceiling: 49,200 ft.
Armament: 36,000 lb. bomb load, including cruise missiles

Future Bombers

The next generation of bomber and strike aircraft is already in development. These planes will have better stealth technology, improved defenses, and increased firepower. Smaller, lighter strike aircraft will replace heavy bombers. There will also be greater use of unmanned aircraft.

New Striker

JOINT STRIKE FIGHTER

The Lockheed Martin Joint Strike Fighter is being developed. It will take over ground attack missions performed by airplanes like the A10 Thunderbolt II. It will be operated by the U.S. Air Force, Navy, and Marine Corps, as well as by allied nations.

The New Heavies

Future replacements for the U.S. long-range bomber fleet are already being planned. A team of leading U.S. aircraft manufacturers are working on two programs for the 2030s. One is supersonic. The other is hypersonic (several times the speed of sound). The supersonic B3 will be a development of the B2 Spirit concept. The aircraft will be able to operate at very high speeds and altitudes. This capability will place it beyond the reach of current anti-aircraft missile technology.

QUIET BOOM

The **supercruise** B3, shown dropping a bomb, will be constructed of space-age materials. Its design will enable it fly at supersonic speeds without a loud **sonic boom**.

UNCONVENTIONAL DESIGN

The hypersonic concept will operate at speeds well beyond the sound barrier, with an all-digital, video-based cockpit. It will look as unworldly as the F117 and B2 when they first appeared. It may ride on "waves" near the edge of space.

>> **sonic boom** = a loud noise made by aircraft passing the sound barrier

Future Bombers

Stealth airplane technology will be increasingly important in the years ahead. Low-level, low-visibility strike aircraft will take on strike missions previously carried out by planes that are easily identified by radar.

STEALTHIER

The F117 Nighthawk, although labeled as a fighter, is very effective as a radar-invisible strike airplane. It was particularly successful during night operations against Iraq's heavily defended capital city of Baghdad in 1991.

>> **intelligence** = information about enemy plans or action

PREDATOR WITHOUT PILOT

The Predator unmanned aerial vehicle (UAV) has been tested as an attack plane, using Hellfire air-to-ground missiles. Many people believe that unmanned combat aerial vehicles (UCAVs) will eventually take over from the crewed bomber. This is likely to be especially true in battle zones remote from the main base.

UNMANNED AIRCRAFT

UAVs provide high-quality local target information and **intelligence**. Better aerial intelligence will improve target accuracy and help to avoid **collateral damage**. This is especially important in operations where terrorist forces are able to mingle with the local population.

EVADER PROJECT

The Evader UAV is testing the suitability of UAVs for high-level reconnaissance missions.

BAE SYSTEMS

EVADER

Hardware at a Glance

AA = anti-aircraft

AIM = air interception missile

ECM = electronic countermeasures

FSA = Future Strike Aircraft

GPS = Global Positioning System

IFF = identification friend or foe

JDAM = Joint Direct Attack Munition

LGB = laser-guided bomb

MAD = Mutually Assured Destruction

MRCA = multirole combat aircraft

NATO = North Atlantic Treaty Organization

SAM = surface-to-air missile

UAV = unmanned aerial vehicle

UCAV = unmanned combat aerial vehicle

VTOL = vertical takeoff and landing

Further Reading & Websites

Angelucci, Enzo. *The Illustrated Encyclopedia of Military Aircraft.* New York: Book Sales, 2001.

Berliner, Don. *Stealth Fighters and Bombers.* Berkeley Heights, NJ: Enslow Publishing, 2001.

Chant, Christopher. *The Role of the Fighter & Bomber.* Broomall, PA: Chelsea House, 1999.

Emert, Phyllis Raybin. *Transports and Bombers (Wild Wings Series).* New York: Julian Messner, 1990.

Ethell, Jeffrey L. *B-17 Flying Fortress.* Osceola, WI: Motorbooks, 1995

Fitzpatrick, Kevin J. *Flying Gunship: the AC-130 Specter.* Chicago, IL: Children's Press, 2000

Holden, Henry M. *Air Force Aircraft (Aircraft).* Berkeley Heights, NJ: Enslow Publishing, 2001.

Holden, Henry M. *Navy Combat Aircraft and Pilots (Aircraft).* Berkeley Heights, NJ: Enslow Publishing, 2002.

Jenssen, Hans. *Look Inside Cross-Sections: Jets.* New York: DK Publishing, 1996.

Loves, June. *Military Aircraft (Flight).* Broomall, PA: Chelsea House, 2001.

Norman, C.J. *Combat Aircraft.* London: Franklin Watts, 1990.

Rendall, David. *Jane's Aircraft Recognition Guide.* New York: HarperCollins, 1999.

Spick, Mike. *B1B (Modern Fighting Aircraft, Vol 11).* New York: Simon & Schuster,1986.

Sweetman, Bill. *Inside the Stealth Bomber (Colortech Series).* Osceola, WI: Motorbooks, 1999

Taylor, Mike. *Air Forces of World War II (World War II).* Edina, MN: Abdo & Daughters, 1998.

Air Force Link <http://www.af.mil>

Center of Military History <http://www.army.mil/cmh-pg>

Commemorative Air Force <http://www.commemorativeairforce.org>

DefenseLink <http://www.defenselink.mil>

Federation of American Scientists <http://www.fas.org/man.index.html>

Military History Online <http://www.militaryhistoryonline.com>

NATO multimedia <http://www.nato.int>

U.S. Marine Corps <http://www.usmc.mil>

U.S. Navy <http://www.navy.mil>

Places to Visit

You can see examples of some of the bombers and strike airplanes contained in this book by visiting the military museums listed here.

American Airpower Heritage Museum, Midland, TX <www.airpowermuseum.org>
Army Aviation Museum, Fort Rucker, Ozark, AL <www.armyavnmuseum.org>
Canadian Warplane Heritage Museum, Hamilton Airport, Mount Hope, Ontario
   <www.warplane.com>
Kenosha Military Museum, Pleasant Prairie, WI <www.kenoshamilitarymuseum.com>
Mighty Eight Air Force Heritage Museum, Pooler, GA <www.mighty8thmuseum.com>
National Museum of Naval Aviation, Pensacola, FL <www.naval-air.org>
Old Rhinebeck Aerodrome, Rhinebeck, NY <www.oldrhinebeck.org>
RCAF Memorial Museum, Trenton, Ontario <www.rcafmuseum.on.ca>
San Diego Aerospace Museum, San Diego, CA <www.aerospacemuseum.org>
Smithsonian National Air and Space Museum, Washington, DC <www.nasm.si.edu>
U.S. Air Force Museum, Wright-Patterson AFB, OH <www.wpafb.af.mil/museum/>
Valiant Air Command Warbird Museum, Titusville, FL <www.vacwarbirds.org>
War Eagles Air Museum,Santa Teresa, NM <www.war-eagles-air-museum.com>
Western Canada Aviation Museum, Winnipeg, Manitoba <www.wcam.mb.ca>

Index

Picture Sources

BAe; 29 (t), 39 (t), 45 (b)
Corel; 20
Defense Visual Information Center: 8 (b), 9, 10, 11 (b),12, 13 (t), 14, 16, 17, 19 (t), 24 (t), 25 (t), 28 (b), 29 (b), 31 (t, b), 32, 33 (t, b), 34 (t), 35 (b), 36, 37, 38
Embraer; 40

Robert Hunt Library; 5, 6, 7 (t), 11 (t), 13 (t), 15, 21, 22, 23, 27 (t), 30,
U.S. Air Force; 4, 7 (b), 10, 13, 15, 18, 19 (b), 24 (b), 25 (b), 26, 33 (t), 39 (b), 41 (b), 42, 43, 44, 45 (t)
U.S. Army; 31 (c)
U.S. Navy; 40–41